God Made FiSH

written by Yvonne Patterson

illustrated by Heidi Petach

Library of Congress Catalog Card No. 85-62951

© 1986. The STANDARD PUBLISHING Company, Cincinnati, Ohio
Division of STANDEX INTERNATIONAL Corporation. Printed in U.S.A.

God made the goldfish, swimming in a bowl,

and the fish you catch with a fishing pole.

He made the sharks,

the stingrays, too,

and placed them in the ocean blue.

Some fish can walk.

Some can even fly.

But my favorite fish are those you fry!

Some can be pets, smaller than puppies.
A good kind to raise are colorful guppies.

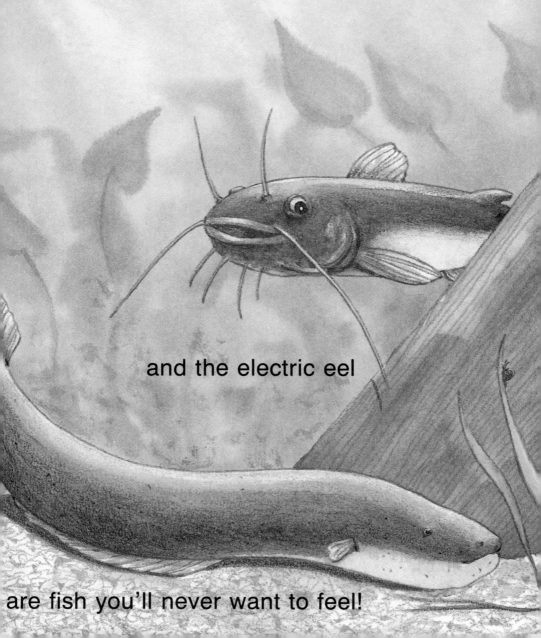

But the whiskered catfish

and the electric eel

are fish you'll never want to feel!

God made the salmon

and the rainbow trout.

They like to swim and jump about.

The sea horse was also made by the Lord.

And He gave one kind of fish, a sword!

Once, long ago, something happened to a man.
   He was swallowed by a fish,
      then spit out on land.
t happened to Jonah because he didn't obey,
   and thought that he could run away.

Once Jesus' disciples had fished all night
   without getting even one little bite.
Jesus told them to try once more,
   before they landed on the sandy shore.
They obeyed Jesus, and what do you think?
   The net was so full, the boat started to sink!

Later Jesus surprised the men once again
by saying, "I'll make you fishers of men.
You won't be catching many fish," He said.
"You'll be bringing people to me, instead!"

Peter's taxes were due, and he was broke.
"Peter, go fishing," was what Jesus spoke.

eter was glad Jesus' words he had heeded.
In a fish's mouth was the money he needed!

Once Jesus' disciples met a happy young lad,
  who offered to share
    the small lunch that he had.
It was only two fish and five loaves of bread.
  But when Jesus prayed, 5,000 were fed!

From scales to tails, from gills to fins,
God made fish, every fish that swims.